Saving Dad

Written by Mary-Anne Creasy

Illustrated by Meredith Thomas

Flying Start
to Literacy®

Contents

Chapter 1:
Disaster on the farm

Dad and Abbey were riding on their motorbike, looking for some lost cows on their farm. They were a long way from their house. Their dog, Sam, was running along behind them.

Then Abbey saw some cows that were stuck down by the river.

"Let's go get them, Sam," yelled Dad.

"Hop off the bike, Abbey," said Dad.
"It will be easier to go down to get
the cows by myself."

As Dad turned to go down to the river,
he fell off his motorbike and it landed
on top of him.

Abbey ran down to him.
"Are you okay, Dad?" she asked.

"I think my leg is broken!" said Dad.

Abbey tried to lift the motorbike off
her dad, but it was too heavy.

Chapter 2: Getting help

Abbey was scared. She knew she had to get help.

"I'll send Sam home to get help, Dad," she said. "I wish I had some paper so that I could write a message to tell the others where we are. Then I could tie the message to his collar."

"It's okay, Abbey. Sam will go home. Mum will know something is wrong when he comes home without us," said Dad.

Abbey pointed in the direction of the house. "Go home, Sam," said Abbey. "Go on. GO HOME!"

Sam barked and ran off towards their farm.

When Sam had gone, Dad and Abbey talked about what they could do next.

"We need to let Mum know where we are," said Abbey. "I'll go and light a small fire on top of that hill so she can see the smoke from the house."

Chapter 3:
Abbey shows the way

Abbey got some matches from the backpack and climbed up to the top of the hill.

Soon she had a fire going. Then she put some green leaves and green grass on the fire so that it would be very smoky. Abbey ran back to Dad.

Abbey started to get worried.
"Dad, we have been gone all afternoon," she said. "The sun is going down and soon it will be dark. What will we do if they can't find us?"

"Listen!" said Dad. "I can hear a truck. I think someone is coming!"

"But they won't know where we are. They won't know to look behind this hill," said Abbey. "We need another way to show them where we are."

Abbey took off her red jacket and tied it to a big stick to make it look like a flag.

Chapter 4:
Abbey makes some noise

Abbey quickly ran to the side of the hill.

She could see some people on horses and some people in a truck, too. They were all going around the other side of the hill.

Then she frantically waved her jacket
like a flag and yelled.
"Help! Help! We are over here! Help!"

But the people in the truck and on
the horses didn't see the red jacket.

She ran back to Dad.
"They still don't know where we are.
I think we need to make some
more noise," she said.

Dad shouted, "Help! Help!"

"They can't hear you!" said Abbey.
"They are too far away."

Abbey grabbed a stick and hit the front
of the motorbike. It made a loud noise
and sounded like a drum. Dad honked
the horn and Abbey banged and banged.

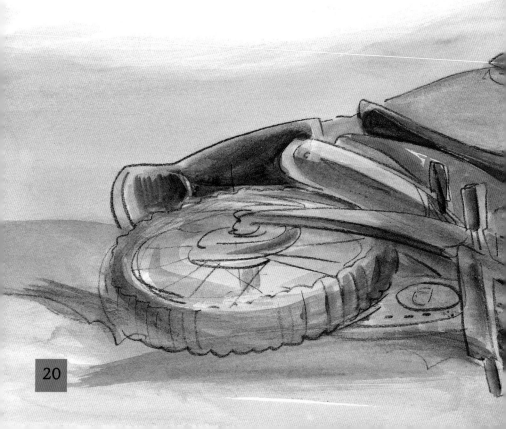

Chapter 5: Sam to the rescue

Then suddenly they could hear barking. Sam came running around the hill, leading everyone to Dad and Abbey.

Sam had saved them.

A note from the author

Today most people have mobile phones and we expect to be able to contact people wherever we are. I wanted to show that in our modern world, in an emergency, we still might need to know how to send messages. But I had to write about a realistic situation showing how messages can be sent using what is around us.

Farmers often travel a long way from their home, checking stock. They can be in remote locations far away from normal communication. Abbey saves her dad using methods that have been around for thousands of years.